Joseph Harrison

The Iron Worker and King Solomon

Vol. 1

Joseph Harrison

The Iron Worker and King Solomon
Vol. 1

ISBN/EAN: 9783337317942

Printed in Europe, USA, Canada, Australia, Japan

Cover: Foto ©ninafisch / pixelio.de

More available books at **www.hansebooks.com**

THE IRON WORKER

AND

KING SOLOMON.

BY

JOSEPH HARRISON, Jr.

WITH A MEMOIR AND AN APPENDIX.

"Behold, I have created the smith, that bloweth the coals in the fire, and that bringeth forth an instrument for his work."—Isaiah, liv. 16.

SECOND EDITION, REVISED.

PRINTED FOR PRIVATE CIRCULATION.

PHILADELPHIA.
J. B. LIPPINCOTT & CO.
1869.

Dedication.

TO THEE,

WHO HAST BEEN

FOR MORE THAN HALF MY LIFE,

MY TRUEST FRIEND,

MY COUNSELOR,

MY WIFE.

TO MY DEAR CHILDREN AND GRANDCHILDREN.

I HAVE written the verses in this little volume, entitled the "IRON WORKER AND KING SOLOMON," for your amusement and instruction, and to impress upon your minds the value of what is but too frequently thought to be very humble labor. The narrative fairly illustrates the Photograph, taken from a picture which, as you know, I value very much, and which you all admire, called the "IRON WORKER," painted for me four or five years ago by Christian Schnessele. The story from which the picture is painted will be found at page 41 of the Appendix, in which will also be found another version of the story of "The Blacksmith and King Solomon," furnished to me by my friend, Mr. Charles G. Leland, who wrote the verses at the close of the book. I am indebted to Mrs. Sarah J. Hale for a corrected copy of her beautiful poem called "IRON," printed in the Appendix. This poem was entirely unknown to me until within a few days.

It has been said by some one that the story of the humblest life, if faithfully written, would prove both

interesting and instructive. As mine has had some
unusual phases, I think it will not look like vanity or
egotism on my part, if I reproduce the Memoir here.
It must always be interesting to all who are so near
to me as yourselves.

Yours ever affectionately,

JOSEPH HARRISON, JR.

Rittenhouse Square, Philadelphia, Christmas, 1867.

CONTENTS.

2

THE IRON WORKER

FROM A PICTURE PAINTED BY CHRISTIAN SCHUSSELE

In the possession of Joseph Harrison, Jr., Philadelphia

THE IRON WORKER

KING SOLOMON.

I.

Adown the street the Blacksmith strode,
  As to his home he went;
His brawny chest heaved to and fro,
  His brow with rage was bent

II

His threshold reached, he entered in,
  His wife and child came near,
But heedless of their greetings kind,
  He muttered, "I'll be there!"

III.

He sat him down in sullen mood,
  Still clouded was his brow;
His wife with anxious look breathed out—
  "There's some great harm, I trow'

IV

"Husband! what wouldst thou? art thou wronged,
    That thus with glower and gloom,
From out thy firm-set clenchéd teeth,
    Thy thoughts in anger come?

V

"Tell me I pray thee.   Calm my fears,
    As I thy meal prepare;
Speak! break my deep solicitude."
    He muttered, "I'll be there!"

VI.

"Where wouldst thou be, my husband, say?
    What is 't that moves thee so?
Is 't aught that I can aid thee in?
    What wouldst thou have me do?

VII

"Thou answerest not, art moody yet;
    Untouched the meal I've laid;
And knotted is thy forehead still;
    In sooth I'm sore afraid

VIII

"That some untoward ill or mischance
  Hath caused thee great dismay
Oh, speak, my husband, tell me all,
  And drive my fears away."

IX

Sadly his eyes were lifted up,
  Sadly his speech began,
And all attent, his good-wife heard,
  As thus his story ran:

X

"Dost thou not know that our Great King
  To-morrow opens wide,
The portals of the Temple rare,
  His glory and his pride?

XI

"The GREAT JEHOVAH willed it all,
  And naught remains, I ween,
Save its solemn consecration,
  Which comes at morning's sheen

XII

"Hast thou not heard who, of the rite
    Are honored by the K
Summoned in full insignia,
    To the sacred opening

XIII

"Of the noblest Sanctuary
    E'er made by human hands,
As now in finished excellence,
    Before the world it stands?

XIV

"The Architect, the Carpenter,
    All cunning in their art,
Surveyor, Mason, Draughtsman, too,
    Are each to take a part.

XV

"And though we hail the wisest King
    That eyes have ever seen,
The wit of world-wise Solomon
    Is now at fault, I ween.

XVI

"At fault in having slighted me,
 'Mongst those who did their best
To rear this peerless wonder-work,
 To fill the King's behest,

XVII

"'Twas I, the now neglected Smith,
 In grimy suit bedight,
Who fashioned curious Instruments,
 To build this Fane aright.—

XVIII

"Without which, those who now are placed
 Above me,—and apart,
All helpless would have found themselves,
 Mere children in their art,

XIX

"From first to last, at morn and night,
 Beside them I've been seen,
And lacking me, and what I've made,
 This Temple ne'er had been

XX

"They say that I ne'er carved in Stone,
    Gold,—Silver,—Bronze, ne'er wrought,
Nor made rare things in Cedar wood,
    From Mount Libanus brought.

XXI.

"That all I've done, is humble work,
    Mere labor of the hand,
Nor Mind nor Science needed. It
    No honor can demand.

XXII.

"And that I am unworthy deemed
    To aid in what's to be.
In all things I too humble seem,
    For this great pageantry.

XXIII

"I tell thee, Art-proud Architect,
    I tell thee, Carpenter,
I tell ye all, ye craft-proud men,
    Unbidden, I'll be there!"

XXIV.

The morrow's sun came glinting o'er
    Tower, obelisk, and plain,
Came with the sun vast multitudes
    To view the hallowed Fane.

XXV.

And Salem's streets were full that morn,
    To see the fair array,
As onward to the Temple gates
    It bent its glittering way.

XXVI.

The doors were opened, entered then
    The King, with heralds bright.
With guards, with all that showed his power,
    In gaudiest hues bedight.

XXVII.

Came Priests in Holy vestments clad,
    With Sacred Ark up-borne,
While fragrant incense curled around,
    In the pure breeze of morn.

XXVIII.

Came Beauty, singing as she went,
　　To harps that filled the air
With sweetest music,—and more loud,
　　The trumpets' distant blare.

XXIX.

In sooth 'twas glorious to behold,
　　Such pageant ne'er had been,
And since that hour, in all the world
　　Its like has not been seen.

XXX.

Through lofty halls, in splendor decked
　　With cedar and with gold,
O'er polished floors, down marble aisles,
　　Their onward way they hold.

XXXI.

The dais is reached, where now the King
　　His regal seat would take,
From whence, in well-appointed phrase,
　　His royal speech would make.

XXXII

The curtain raised, strange sight is seen,
    For next the chiefest seat,
Sits, in defiant attitude,
    A figure all unmeet.

XXXIII.

His head is bare, his brow is grimed,
    Bare are his arms and chest;
A leathern garment hides his limbs,
    His hand on hammer rests.

XXXIV.

"Whence came this hind?" "What doth he there?"
    Was passed from man to man;
With threatening looks, with flashing steel,
    The guards full at him ran.

XXXV.

"Tear down the caitiff!" "Rend him sore!
    Sure he no mercy needs!"
Still there he sits, in conscious pride,
    Nor sword nor clamor heeds.

XXXVI.

"Hold!" cries the King; "nor do him ill,
  Mayhap he can explain
Why thus he comes unbidden here
  Amidst our glittering train.

XXXVII.

"Speak freely, man, heed not my power,
  Full justice thou shalt share,
If thou canst show in very truth
  Why thou art sitting there."

XXXVIII.

"All hail! Great King, forever live!"
  Thus spake the intruding guest;
"Hear me, O hear thy servant's words,
  Then urge thy high behest.

XXXIX.

"I do not sit unbidden here,
  I came but at thy call;
Though not amongst the honored ones,
  I'm not the least of all.

XL.

"Didst not, O King, ask here to-day,
     All those who most have done
This marvelous work that round us glows,
     In this bright morning's sun?

XLI.

"Hast thou not asked the Architect,
     Surveyor, Mason, those
Under whose skillful, cunning arts
     This wondrous Temple rose.

XLII.

"The world doth hail thee wisest King
     That eyes have ever seen,
Yet the wit of mighty Solomon
     May be at fault, I ween.

XLIII.

"For thou hast overlooked the SMITH,
     Whose ever-needed skill,
In modest labor aided most
     Thy royal wish to fill.

XLIV

"Ask these who stand round thee to-day,
    Above me, placed apart,
If they all helpless had not been
    But for my curious art.

XLV.

"To thee I turn, proud Architect;
    Canst thou my words gainsay?
I speak to all ye craft-proud men,
    Come, answer as ye may.

XLVI.

"Ye know that I, from first to last,
    Your surest aid have been;
Lacking my IRON Instruments,
    This Temple none had seen.

XLVII.

" I wait reply."—With eagle glance,
    The Blacksmith looked around,
His rivals in the King's regard,
    Their eyes fixed on the ground,

XLVIII.

Nor uttered word. "What! no response?
    Great King, O live for e'er!
Have I not shown in very truth
    Why I am sitting here?"

XLIX

King Solomon a lesson read,
    And for a moment mused,
Spake to the Smith in kindly word,
    "Thou hast been much abused.

L.

"Stay where thou art a moment: let
    All those who thee contemn,
Receive with me thy just rebuke:
    Thou art the best of them.

LI.

"Then haste to get thee clean attire,
    Then haste to make thee neat:
For at the royal feast to-day,
    Thou'lt fill the right-hand seat."

LII

The Smith a brief space sat erect.
    Then o'er his shoulder threw
His faithful hammer. Justified,
    He quietly withdrew.

LIII

The people shout: King Solomon
    His royal speech did end;
The Temple's consecration o'er,
    The throng all homeward wend.——

LIV.

Adown the street the Blacksmith goes,
    How changed from yesterday!
No more in sullen mood doth he
    Pursue his onward way.

LV.

His threshold reached, he enters in,
    Not now with brow of care.
But with exulting voice exclaims.
    "I told thee I'd be there!"

LVI.

His wife in mute amazement clings
  Close to his side the while:
His little boy looks up in fear,
  And meets his father's smile.

LVII.

"Greet me, ye loved ones, greet me well.
  Join me in glad acclaim,
The Blacksmith now has justice won!
  He'll ne'er be scorned again!

LVIII.

"Get me, good wife, my best attire,
  Help me to make me neat:
I DINE with our great King to-day.
  I fill the honored seat."

LIX.

Then spake the wife: "I feared this morn
  That thy determined will,
Might lead thee to assert thy right,
  And bring thee grievous ill.

LX.

"I, to the Temple trembling went,
  And saw thee sitting proud;
I saw the naked steel gleam out,
  I heard the tumult loud.

LXI.

"But ere our Monarch interposed,
  To stay the impending blow,
I, to the earth in terror fell,
  And nothing more did know

LXII.

"Till at our humble roof once more,
  I waked to conscious thought,
And met the smiles of kindly friends,
  Who homeward me had brought.

LXIII.

"But thou art saved, art honored, too;
  Let all our thanks ascend
To Him, who stands our sure firm rock,
  Our ever-constant friend!"

The wisdom of King Solomon.

Is still our highest praise;

The Blacksmith has his full reward.

As in the ancient days.

MEMOIR.

MÉMOIR.

[Reprinted from Bishop's History of American Manufactures, 1866.

JOSEPH HARRISON, JR., whose successful enterprise at home and abroad has made his name a familiar one to the manufacturers of two continents, was born in the district of the Northern Liberties, now a part of the Consolidated City of Philadelphia, on September 20th, 1810;* and at the age of fifteen was indentured an apprentice to the art of machine-making—a trade that he had himself selected. A foreman at twenty in the shop in which he had served his time, he commenced life at twenty-one with a fair knowledge of his craft, correct industrious habits, but with little chance, apparently, or expectation of special preferment, except in the usual routine of his calling.

Employed in several prominent machine shops of that day, and as foreman for Messrs. Garrett and Eastwick, he in 1837 became associated in partnership with these gentlemen in the manufacture of locomotive engines. This firm, soon changed to Eastwick and Harrison, were the originators of several important improvements, that have

* The house in which the subject of this memoir was born, stood, up to 1831, on Noble street near the N. W. corner of Front street. It was built anterior to 1752.

32   MEMOIR.

contributed to the present perfection of the American locomotive. In their hands the eight-wheel engine, with four driving and four truck wheels, was first brought into a practicable shape. It is now almost exclusively used in this country for passenger trains, and is obtaining a sure and steady reputation in Europe. The present modes of equalizing the weight on the driving wheels, indispensable to this engine, were patented by Joseph Harrison, Jr., the subject of this notice, in 1839, and are now applied by all the manufacturers of locomotive engines in this country.

In 1841 a locomotive called the *"Gowan and Marx,"* weighing but little over eleven tons, was designed and built by this firm for the Philadelphia and Reading Railroad.

The performance of this engine in drawing *one hundred and one* loaded coal-cars over that road, attracted great attention at the time, as being without a parallel in the history of railroad transportation. Locomotives, designed and built by Eastwick and Harrison for the Beaver Meadow, Hazleton and Sugar Loaf Railroads, burned anthracite coal successfully as early as 1835 and 1836, and in a regular freight business over these roads, surmounted higher grades than had ever been practically overcome in this country or in Europe.

In 1840, Colonel Melnikoff and Colonel Kraft, two eminent engineers, were sent to this country by the Russian Government to examine and report upon the American Railway System, with a view to its adoption in that Empire. The reputation already acquired by the firm of Eastwick and Harrison attracted their attention, and induced these gentlemen on their return to Russia to propose that Mr. Harrison should be sent for to undertake the construction of the locomotives and rolling stock for the St. Petersburg and Moscow Railway, a road more than four hundred miles long, then about being commenced under the direction of an eminent American, Major George W. Whistler, who had been called to Russia in 1842 as Consulting Engineer of the Railway Department of the Russian Government.

In the spring of 1843 Mr. Harrison embarked for Europe, and in December of that year, he, in association with his partner in Philadelphia, Mr. Eastwick, and Mr. Thomas Winans, of Baltimore, concluded a contract with the Russian Government, amounting to three millions of dollars, the work to be completed in five years. It was a condition that this work was all to be done at St. Petersburg, by Russian workmen, or such as could be found on the spot.

With workmen entirely unacquainted with the work to be done, and without knowing the language or the peculiar manner of doing business in a foreign land, Messrs. Harrison, Winans and Eastwick, the new firm established at St. Petersburg, set about the difficult, and to almost every one but themselves, the impossible task of complying with the terms of their contract.

Commencing their business in the straightforward manner they had pursued at home, they asked only not to be hindered, and so well were their plans arranged and carried out, that all the work contracted for was completed to the entire satisfaction of the Russian Government, and paid for, more than one year before the terms of the contract had expired.

During the progress of this work, other orders, reaching to nearly two millions of dollars, were added to the original amount, including the completion of the great Cast Iron Bridge over the River Neva, at St. Petersburg, the largest and most costly structure of the kind in the world. To complete this structure, another year was added to the original term of the first contract.

Before the close of the first term, a second contract was made for a further period of twelve years, for maintaining in running order, the rolling stock of the St. Petersburg and Moscow Railway. The parties to this contract being Joseph Harrison, Jr., Thomas Winans, and William L. Winans. This second contract was carried on, and finished to the satisfaction of both parties in 1862. During the year just mentioned, a contract was made with a French company for maintaining the rolling stock of the St. Petersburg and Moscow Railway.

This company commenced their work with the machinery in such perfect order, as was not perhaps to be found on any railway of similar length in the world. From this perfection, with all the workshops, tools, and other arrangements ready to their hands, which their predecessors had been twelve years in bringing to completeness, the rolling stock was so much run down in three years, as to compel an abrupt termination of the French company's contract by the government. A new contract was made in 1865 with Mr. Thomas Winans and Mr.

William L. Winans, who were then in Europe, for another term of eight years.

It will thus be seen that American reputation in railway mechanical engineering, first begun in Philadelphia, by Mr. Harrison and his partner, in their intercourse with Colonel Melnikoff and Colonel Kraft, in 1840, has since maintained itself in Russia against all comers, and has now no competitor.

In 1847, the Emperor Nicholas, accompanied by his second son the Grand Duke Constantine, Prince Paskewitch, Viceroy of Poland, with all the high officers of the Russian Government, visited the Alexandroffsky Head Mechanical Works of the St. Petersburg and Moscow Railway, where the work for the road was being done.

After spending many hours in a minute examination of the establishment in every part, the Emperor offering his hand at parting to the American contractors, and thanking them, expressed the greatest satisfaction at what had been shown and explained to him. As an additional mark of his approval, his Majesty sent to each of our countrymen engaged in the firm, most beautiful rings, set with diamonds, of a present value of not less than three thousand dollars each.

On the occasion of the opening of the Neva Bridge, in the autumn of 1850, then just completed, the Emperor Nicholas, as a further mark of esteem, bestowed upon Mr. Harrison the ribbon of the Order of St. Anne, with a massive gold medal attached thereto. On the superior side of the medal is a portrait of his Majesty, the reverse side having the motto, in the Russian language, "For Zeal."

In 1852 Mr. Harrison returned to Philadelphia, and set about employing the means that had rewarded his enterprise abroad, for the adornment of his native city. He erected numerous and costly buildings, some with original features, not heretofore seen in this country; and established the most extensive, and probably the first private gallery of Art in Philadelphia.

Though twelve years of the last twenty of his life have been spent abroad, it is evident that he has not lost affection for the place of his birth, or forgotten the duties of a public-spirited citizen.

Early in his engineering life, Mr. Harrison's attention was directed to the means of improving steam generation, more particularly with a view of making this powerful agent less dangerous, and less liable to explosion. The result of his efforts in this direction is now before the public in his most original "Harrison Steam Boiler," now largely coming into use. The first boiler made on this improved principle was put in operation at Messrs. William Sellers & Co.'s works in 1859, and supplied steam for their entire establishment for several months in the summer of that year.

Mr. Harrison's first patent for the Harrison Boiler is dated October 4th, 1859, though improvements on the original idea have since been the subject of several patents in this country and in Europe.

At the International Exhibition, held in London in

1862, the highest class medal was awarded to this boiler, "*for originality of design and general merit.*"

Mr. Harrison is now pursuing, with the zeal and perseverance of his earlier life, the highly important object of making steam generation safe from its present destructiveness to life and property. He is aiming at a complete revolution in the form and material of the present system. Success will place him among the benefactors of our race.

THE CRUCIFIXION.

Written in a Lady's Album, in 184

BY JOSEPH HARRISON JR.

WHAT means yon sad procession onward wending,
  With measured tread, up Calvary's Mountain side?
What mean those vast assembled hosts attending?
  Thousands on thousands swell the living tide

Amidst moves one whose face with love is beaming;
  Bowed to the earth, a heavy cross he bears.
See! o'er his brow the sanguine flood is streaming;
  Pierced are his temples with the crown he wears.

'Tis our loved Saviour they are upward leading;
  To death they bear him on, with ruthless hands;
Fainting and worn, his heart for sinners bleeding,
  Now on the summit, meek and low he stands.

To the dread cross his hands and feet they're nailing;
  Unmurmuring, unresisting, see he yields;
All are relentless, none his fate bewailing,
  Save the sad group that in the distance kneels.

(39)

The cross is raised, is fixed; and now, toward Heaven,
    The Saviour's voice is heard, plaintive and low:
"Father, O Father! be thy pardon given!
    Forgive! forgive! they know not what they do."

Again he speaks; hear his deep accents breathing:
    "'Tis finished; all on earth is done," he cries.
He bows his head; his spirit now is leaving
    Its earthly tenement. He dies! he dies!

All nature mourns; the sun, his rays withholding,
    Spreads gloom around; the Temple's vail is rent;
The dead arise, their cerements unfolding.
    Stricken with fear, the throng in terror went.

Man, cruel man, how couldst thou, in thy blindness,
    Thus vainly strive to thwart thy coming good?
How couldst thou thus repay his every kindness,
    And deeply dye thy hands in precious blood?

Oh! why was this tremendous deed permitted?
    Why was thy hand, O God, uplifted still?
'Twas this: by it were all our sins remitted;
    'Twas done, obedient to Jehovah's will

APPENDIX.

REMARKS OF JOSEPH HARRISON, JR.,

At the Public Dinner given to Henry C. Carey, Esq., at the La Pierre House, Philadelphia, April 27th, 1859.

> "Der Gott der Eisen wachsen liess,
> Der wollte keine Knechte,
> Drum gab er Sabel, Schwerdt und Spiess,
> Dem Mann in seine Rechte."
>
> A. METTERNISSEL.

> "The Lord, who made hard iron grow,
> Ne'er wished to see a slave;
> And, therefore, spear and tauldhion true
> To man's right hand he gave."

In attempting to say a few words on the Mechanic Arts, I am sure you will find the task in unworthy, if not in very prejudiced hands.

Webster defines "Mechanic" to be "a person whose occupation is to construct machines, or goods, wares, furniture, and the like." And the "mechanic arts," he says, "are those in which the hands are more concerned than the mind, as in making clothes and utensils." Perhaps no single word in our language embraces a wider field than the one first named, while the latter definition hardly does justice to the term "Mechanic Arts." I think I am right in inferring that the venerable lexicographer was not a mechanic.

The Great Jehovah himself was the first, the Great Mechanic; and when our first parent was compelled to earn his bread in the "sweat of his face," as stern a necessity compelled him to turn mechanic, and he thereby became the first human promoter of the mechanic arts. Adam could not till the ground with his bare hands, and we can imagine him pointing a stick against the roughened surface of a stone, and thus, by mechanical means, making the first rude instrument to aid him in his new vocation.

The first altars reared for sacrifice required some mechanical skill to give them form and stability; and are we not told of Tubal Cain, "that he was an instructor of every artificer in brass and iron"? Noah was an eminent mechanic, and promoter of the mechanic arts, as were also those who planned and built the Tabernacle with its holy contents. World-wise Solomon swells the list, with Hiram of Tyre, and all those who so cunningly worked in iron and in brass, in gold and in silver, and in cedar wood, on the holiest and grandest of temples.

Thus, from the fall of man to the present hour, the "Mechanic" and the "Mechanic Arts" have been ministering to our comfort, our conveniences, and to our intelligence in every walk of life, and will thus go on ministering to the end.

That glorious metal, IRON, must ever be the great agent for promoting the mechanic arts. Iron is the true precious metal—a metal so interwoven with the wants of life, and our very enjoyments, that to do without it would be to relapse into barbarism. Take away gold and silver, and the whole range of baser metals, leaving us iron, and we would hardly miss them. Take away Iron, and we lose next to life, and that which sustains life, the greatest boon the Almighty has bestowed upon man.

I need not take up the time of this company by referring to the uses of iron, or how much our necessities, our comforts, and our enjoyments are dependent upon its uses, whether in out-door labor, in the home circle, the manufactory, the hall of science, or the field of art, but I will say a word touching the importance of the worker in iron.

I remember reading a story in my early boyhood, that impressed itself so strongly upon my mind that I have never forgotten it. I wish I could find it now. I do not remember the exact words, but the matter ran somewhat in this wise:

When King Solomon had finished the Temple, and having set apart a day for its consecration, he invited to the ceremony all the great men of the kingdom, together with the Architect, the Surveyor, the Chief Carpenter, the Chief Mason, and others who had been engaged in planning and directing the work.

The vast edifice rested with closed doors awaiting the arrival of the King. He came at length, the doors were opened, and to the sound of tabret, harp, psaltery, and trumpet, the solemn and imposing procession entered the house then to be dedicated to the worship of the living God.

As the King moved toward the seat prepared for him, to the amazement of all, a stalwart Smith was seen sitting on the right-hand seat nearest the throne.

Hammer in hand, bare-armed and head erect, with reeking sweat upon his brow, showing him fresh from the forge, he sate, nothing daunted by the near approach of Majesty. A movement was made to remove the bold intruder. Hold! cried the King, and thus he spake to the Smith: Friend, why art thou here filling a place intended for one better than thou? Mighty King! O! live forever, replied the Smith: I own no superior here, save your Royal Majesty, and I fill this place, as by right it is mine, and as I will presently show if thou wilt graciously permit me. Your Majesty hath invited here to-day the Chief Architect, the Surveyor, the Chief Mason, and many others who have labored herein; but thou hast overlooked the so-thought humble Smith, to whom all these who have been honored with a place at this ceremony are indebted.

Without the Instruments that I had prepared for them, could the Chief Architect make his plans, the Surveyor his lines? Could the Mason carve his stone, or the Carpenter fashion his wood?

The very first stroke in the construction of this great edifice was made by the Smith, and from the beginning unto the end, he has been by the side of those who have built this work, aiding them with his art, in making Instruments without which this Temple could not have been reared.

Solomon mused for a moment, and then said: " Friend, thou speakest but too truly. Much is indeed due to thee, and thou shouldst not have been neglected. Stay where thou art, and let those who would have spurned thee from thy place feel with me the just reward than hast bestowed upon us."

It is even now as in the days of King Solomon: the Worker in Iron — whether in producing it from the ore, as handicraftsman, or one who plans and devises new and useful ways of applying iron for man's comfort and benefit — is, and must ever be, the true promoter of the Mechanic Arts, the benefactor of our race. Before sitting down, I would say a word regarding a branch of the Mechanic Arts which is not sufficiently known and appreciated, except by the few who come in immediate contact with it. Thirty-five years ago (I speak from my own personal knowledge), hammer, chisel, and file, hand-lathe, drill-brace, and screw-stock were almost the only instruments used in working iron, after it came from the foundry and forge. Now, machines are made to fashion iron into almost every form by other than man's power and skill — manual and even mental toil being in a great degree superseded by these machines.

Each workman now does fully the work of five, as compared with thirty-five years ago, and with such accuracy as never was attained by the hand worker.

To be proficient in the use of these machines does not require the old-fashioned seven years' apprenticeship, as intelligent men, whether brought up to mechanical trades or not, soon acquire proficiency in their use.

Without these improvements, in working and fashioning iron, the vast demand which has sprung up within the last thirty years in every shape and form, from the mammoth

steamship to the tiny sewing machine, could not have been
supplied. Skilled workmen in the branches of steam machinery alone, could not have been raised up fast enough to
do one-quarter of what has been done in the development
of the railroad, steam navigation, and the thousand other ob-
jects in which steam is now used. All these great results
have been secured almost entirely by the use of that most
noble metal, iron.

Our city has long been celebrated by its superior products
in iron — in our locomotive, marine, and stationary engines,
in railway wheels, architectural castings, and the like; but
it is not so well known that we have in our midst the
very best establishments in the country for making engineers'
tools, or rather machines for working iron. I say the best in
this country. I do not fear to say that the tools made here
are equal to the very best made in any country. In no place
have greater improvements been made than here, in this important branch of the mechanic arts.

As a proof of this, our workshops are sending their work
throughout the length of this great land, and are even at
this moment executing large orders for countries far beyond
the sea. I thank you, Mr. Chairman and gentlemen, for your
attention, and will not trespass further upon your time. Iron
has been mainly my theme, than which, connected with the
mechanic arts, I know no nobler one. Heaven forbid that I
should ever bow down to an idol. When I do so, it shall be
made of IRON.

IRON.

BY MRS. HALE.

"Truth shall spring out of the Earth."—Ps. lxxxv. 11.

As in lonely thought I pondered
    On the marv'lous things of earth,
And, in fancy's dreaming, wondered
    At their beauty, power, and worth,
Came, like words of prayer, the feeling—
    Oh! that God would make me know,
Through the Spirit's clear revealing—
    What, of all His work below,
Is to man a boon the greatest,
    Brightening on from age to age,
Serving truest, earliest, latest,
    Through the world's long pilgrimage.

Soon vast mountains rose before me,
    Shaggy, desolate, and lone,
Their scarred heads were threatening o'er me,
    Their dark shadows round me thrown:

Then a Voice from out the mountains,
  As an earthquake shook the ground,
And like frightened fawns the fountains,
  Leaping, fled before the sound;
And the Anak oaks bowed lowly,
  Quivering, aspen-like, with fear,—
While the deep response came slowly,
  Or it must have crushed mine ear—

"Iron! Iron! Iron!"—crashing
  Like the battle-axe and shield;
Or the sword on helmet clashing
  Through a bloody battle-field!
"Iron! Iron! Iron!"—rolling
  Like the far-off cannon's boom;
Or the death-knell slowly tolling
  Through a dungeon's charnel gloom!
"Iron! Iron! Iron!"—swinging
  As the summer breezes play;
Or as bells of Time were ringing
  In the blest Millennial Day!

Then the clouds of ancient fable
  Cleared away before mine eyes;
Faith could find a footing stable
  O'er the gulf of mysteries!
Words the prophet bards had uttered,
  Signs the oracles foretold,

Spells the weird-like Sibyl muttered
   Through the twilight days of old,
Rightly read, Beneath the splendor
   Shining now on history's page,
All their faithful witness render—
   All portend a better age.

Sisyphus, forever toiling,
   Was the type of toiling men,
While the stone of power, recoiling,
   Crashed them back to earth again:
Stern Prometheus, bound and bleeding,
   Imaged man in mental chain,
While the vultures, on him feeding,
   Were the passions' vengeful reign;
Still a ray of mercy tarried,
   On the cloud, a white-winged dove,
For this mystic faith had married
   Vulcan to the Queen of Love!

Rugged strength and radiant beauty—
   These were one in Nature's plan;
Humble toil and Heavenward duty—
   These will form the perfect man;—
Darkly was this doctrine taught us
   By the gods of heathendom,
But the living light was brought us
   When the Gospel morn had come:

How the glorious change, expected,
  Could be wrought, was then made free;
Of the earthly, when perfected,
  Rugged Iron forms the key!

"Truth from out the earth shall flourish,"
  This the Word of God makes known—
Thence are harvests men to nourish—
  There let Iron's power be shown.
Of the swords, from slaughter gory,
  Ploughshares forge to break the soil;
Then will Mind attain its glory,
  Then will Labor reap the spoil.—
Error cease the soul to wilder,
  Crime be checked by simple good,
As the little coral builder
  Forces back the furious flood

While our faith in good grows stronger,
  Means of greater good increase:
Iron, slave of War no longer,
  Leads the onward march of Peace;
Still new modes of service finding,
  Ocean, earth, and air it moves,
And the distant nations binding,
  Like the kindred tie it proves;
With its Atlas-shoulder sharing
  Loads of human toil and care;

On its wing of lightning bearing
   Thought's swift mission through the air

As the rivers, farthest flowing,
   In the highest hills have birth;
As the banyan, broadest growing,
   Oftenest bows its head to earth.—
So the mightiest minds press onward
   Channels free of good to trace;
So the holiest hearts bend downward,
   Circling all the human race;
Thus by Iron's aid pursuing
   Through the earth their plans of love,
Men our Father's will are doing
   Here, as angels do above.

THE BLACKSMITH

AND

KING SOLOMON.

A RABBINICAL LEGEND.

———◦◦———

AND it came to pass when Solomon, the son of David, had finished the Temple of Jerusalem, that he called unto him the chief architects, the head artificers, and cunning men working in silver and gold, and in wood, and in ivory and stone,—yea, all who aided in working on the Temple of the Lord, and he said to them:

Sit ye down at my table, for I have prepared a feast for all my chief workers and artificers. Stretch forth your hands, therefore, and eat and drink and be merry. Is not the laborer worthy of his hire? Is not the skillful artificer deserving of honor? Muzzle not the ox that treadeth out the corn.

And when Solomon and the chief workmen were seated, and the fatness of the land and the oil thereof were upon the table, there came one who knocked loudly upon the door, and forced himself even into the festal chamber. Then Solomon the King was wroth, and said: What manner of man art thou?

And the man answered and said: When men wish to honor me, they call me Son of the Forge, but when they desire to mock me, they call me Blacksmith; and seeing that the toil of working in fire covers me with sweat, the latter name, O! King, is not inapt, and in truth I desire no better.

But, said Solomon: Why comest thou thus rudely and unbidden to the feast, where none save the chief workmen of the Temple are invited?

And the man replied: Please ye, I came rudely because the servant obliged me to force my way; but I came not unbidden. Was it not proclaimed that the chief workmen of the Temple are invited to dine with the King of Israel?

Then he who carved the cherubim said: This fellow is no sculptor.

And he who inlaid the roof with pure gold said: Neither is he a worker in fine metals.

And he who raised the walls said: He is not a cutter of stone.

And he who made the roof cried out: He is not cunning in cedar wood, neither knoweth he the mystery of uniting strange pieces of timber together.

Then said Solomon: What hast thou to say, Son of the Forge, why I should not order thee to be plucked by the beard, scourged with a scourge, and stoned to death with stones?

When the Son of the Forge heard this, he was in no sort dismayed, but advancing to the table, snatched up and swallowed a cup of wine, and said:

O! King, live forever! The chief men of the workers in wood and gold and stone have said that I am not of them, and they have said truly. I am their superior. Before they lived I was created. I am their master, and they are all my servants. And he turned him round and said to the chief of the carvers in stone:

Who made the tools with which you carve?

And he said: THE BLACKSMITH.

And he said to the chief of the workers in wood:

Who made the tools with which you hewed the trees of Lebanon, and formed them into pillars and roof for the Temple?

And he said: THE BLACKSMITH.

Then he said to the artificer in gold and ivory:

Who makes your instruments by which you work beautiful things for my Lord, the King?

And he said: THE BLACKSMITH.

Enough, enough, my good fellow, said Solomon; thou hast proved that I invited thee, and that thou art all men's father in art. Go wash the sweat of the forge from thy face, and come and sit at my right hand. The chiefs of my workmen are but men. Thou art more.

So it happened at the feast of Solomon, and Blacksmiths have been honored ever since.

THE BLACKSMITH.

BY CHARLES G. LELAND.

I DREAMED I stood by a roaring fire
  Near the Blacksmith grimy and grim,
And watched the sparks rise higher and higher,
  As it lit up each brawny limb

    Bang, bang, the hammer rang,
      And drove out many a spark,
    They seemed the Devil's own fire-flies,
      As they darted through the dark

The Smith struck high, the Smith struck low,
  As over his work he bent,
And if every blow had been on a foe,
  A battle had soon been spent

    Clang, cling, the steel doth ring,
      In flaming crimson dressed,
    Of all the callings that I know,
      I love the Blacksmith's best

King Siegfried of old was a Blacksmith bold,
  And well on the iron could pound;
With his very first blow he drove, I'm told,
  The anvil into the ground.

        Round, round, into the ground,
          And beat his hammer flat.
        No man alive, but a Blacksmith stout,
          Could strike you a blow like that.

And Siegfried became a monarch of might,
  So you may clearly see,
If a man would rise in power and height,
  A Blacksmith he well may be.

        Smack, smack, with many a crack,
          As he hammers the spade and plough.
        For so did Tubal Cain of old,
          And he must do so now.

                THE END.

www.ingramcontent.com/pod-product-compliance
Lightning Source LLC
Chambersburg PA
CBHW031808090426
42739CB00008B/1217